JUAN LUNA'S REVOLVER

T0323849

THE ERNEST SANDEEN PRIZE IN POETRY

EDITOR

Cornelius Eady

2009, *Juan Luna's Revolver,* Luisa A. Igloria

2007, *The Curator of Silence,* Jude Nutter

2005, *Lives of the Sleepers,* Ned Balbo

2003, *Breeze,* John Latta

2001, *No Messages,* Robert Hahn

1999, *The Green Tuxedo,* Janet Holmes

1997, *True North,* Stephanie Strickland

Juan Luna's
REV✿LVER

LUISA A. IGLORIA

University of Notre Dame Press
Notre Dame, Indiana

Published by the University of Notre Dame Press
Notre Dame, Indiana 46556
www.undpress.nd.edu

Library of Congress Cataloging-in-Publication Data
Igloria, Luisa A., 1961–
Juan Luna's revolver / Luisa A. Igloria.
p. cm. — (The Ernest Sandeen Prize in poetry)
ISBN-13: 978-0-268-03178-7 (pbk. : alk. paper)
ISBN-10: 0-268-03178-9 (pbk. : alk. paper)
1. Filipinos—Poetry.   2. Group identity—Poetry.   I. Title.
PS3553.A686J83   2008
811'.54—dc22

2008027897

∞ *The paper in this book meets the guidelines for permanence and durability of the Committee on Production Guidelines for Book Longevity of the Council on Library Resources.*

For Ruben

And in memoriam:

Gabriel Zafra Aguilar (10 December 1913 – 31 July 1990)

Cresencia Rillera Buccat (14 September 1940 – 5 June 2006)

CONTENTS

Acknowledgments

(Citations, Prizes, and Individual Poems Published in Literary Journals)

"The Clear Bones," 2007 49th Parallel Prize for Poetry, selected by Carolyne Wright, *Bellingham Review*

"Hill Station," in *Language for a New Century: Contemporary Poetry from the Middle East, Asia, and Beyond,* ed. Tina Chang, Ravi Shankar, and Nathalie Handal (W. W. Norton, 2008)

"The Minim," *Natural Bridge* (spring 2008)

"Venom," 2007 James Hearst Poetry Prize, selected by former US Poet Laureate Ted Kooser, *The North American Review* (March–April 2007)

"Mrs. Wilkin Teaches an Igorot the Cakewalk," Finalist, 2007 49th Parallel Prize, *Bellingham Review*

"Intimacy deserves a closer look," Finalist, 2007 Indiana Review Poetry Prize, *Indiana Review* (winter 2007)

"Black Elk," "*Letras y Figuras,*" "Doctrina Christiana," Finalist citation (but not publication), 2007 Lynda Hull Memorial Award for Poetry, *Crazyhorse*

"Descent," 2006 National Writers Union Award for Poetry, selected by Adrienne Rich National Writers Union and *Poetry Flash*

"Rainy Day," "Dolorosa," "Bypass," "Your Hand in My Side," 2006 Richard Peterson Poetry Prize, *Crab Orchard Review* (fall–winter 2006)

"Marine Layer," Finalist, 2006 Muriel Craft Bailey Poetry Prize, *Comstock Review* (fall 2006)

"Sediment," "Wanting," *Smartish Pace* (spring 2006)

"Worth," 2007 *Her Mark Calendar*, Woman Made Gallery, Chicago (winter 2006)

"Blur," *Columbia Poetry Review* (spring 2005)

"Yekaterinsky dvorets, Tsarkovoe Selo," in "Wish You Were Here" Postcard series, *Switched-on Gutenberg* (fall 2003)

Thank you to my students, trusted readers, and enabling friends — Myrna Amelia Mesa, Natalie Diaz, Monique Cover, Andrea Nolan, Joanna Eleftheriou, Mary Hanlin, Stavros Lambrakis, Warren D.M. Reed, Mary-Jean Kledzik, Christian Anton Gerard, Rebecca Lauren and Joseph Gidjunis; Jose Edmundo Ocampo Reyes, Gemino H. Abad, Rocío G. Davis, Gerald Burns, Kristine Fonacier, Gladys Lyn and Pancho Lapuz, Rebecca Añonuevo, Alice M. Sun-Cua, Shirley O. Lua, Elizabeth Lolarga, Reme Antonia Grefalda, Scott Choi, Marianne Villanueva, Aimee Nezhukumatathil, J. L. Rosser, Wang Ping, Sabina Murray, Michael Blumenthal, Alfred Yuson, Reine Marie Melvin, Manolita Farolan Doise, Rochita Loenen-Ruiz, Linda Maria Nietes, Angela Mascareñas, Tom Kelly, Patrick Cole, and Pinky Arce Alinea; to Eugene Gloria and to Vicente L. Rafael (for his book *The Promise of the Foreign: Nationalism and the Technics of Translation in the Spanish Philippines*, Duke University Press, 2005); to the MFA Creative Writing Program and the University Press at the University of Notre Dame. Gratitude always to my families, immediate and extended; to the Ragdale Foundation and Staff for time and ease in the summer of 2006, and for the first Sylvia Clare Brown Fellowship which allowed me to complete work on this manuscript; to the 2005 Napa Valley Writers Conference; and to the 2003 Summer Literary Seminars in St. Petersburg, Russia.

JUAN LUNA'S REVOLVER

JOURNEY TO THE WEST

Opening his brown coat, Monkey shook a hundred jewels to the ground.

They shone, pomegranate seeds in moonlight. They pulled
me under their bright sleeves. Of course I wanted to taste.

The wheel turned in the direction of the sun. Faster than a tail flick
the waters rose. Birds scattered ideographs for change. None of this,

ever meant in malice. Marigold heads bent against a scrim of glass.
The instrument approached its vibrato. The payment for a kiss,

in the tumult— not after, but before.
What did it mean, the dense brocade of grass,

the open gate; the tiller that the hand turned
in another direction? I didn't see the goddess

pulling the line across continents in darkness,
did not see her face, lovely and indifferent;

my cares, a small boat that drifted on water.

I /

INDIOS BRAVOS

INVOCATION

Thin dragées of falling light when I held the entrance
open, made welcome. He smiled and glinted under
the awning of his most polished smile. Is this the enemy,
the dear distraction? I led him in, hung his smooth silks
next to rayons and rain shedders decaying in the closet. Who
would not plump cushions with her own hands, anoint
window-ledges with yellow paste and cinnabar, all night
pour pistachios into each gaping bowl? All the saved copper
clanking in coffers I fed to the feast, all my silver. For it was
months since sweetness had left the water, since moth wings
grazed the burning lamps, sizzling down to papery ash.
When would the compassionate affix his watermark,
his sandal-print upon the page? So I could go on I festooned my lap
with garlands, steeled my neck toward the fire. My muse was my desire.

La indolencia de los Filipinos . . .

INTIMACY DESERVES A CLOSER LOOK

on the boulevards, where a mural assembles nightly.
Bodies the hue of scrap metal beneath train tracks,
feathered by neon. My friend the pathologist walks
back to Manila Hotel, cuts through the park and comes
across lit fires in iron gratings. The third eye
of a Sanyo rice cooker blinks the hours from a billboard.
A man scrubs himself with a pumice stone in the fountain,
a family of four sleeps next to their faded mango trishaw.
So languid even in repose, he writes. Here,
as in that part of the world, the spirit relinquishes itself.
Lizards free-fall to the ground. Bells' tongues rend the Angelus.
But history expounds on the imprecision of Chinese
water-clocks and the industry of Northerners, the brighter
ink of spiked holly berries against white, the augur-shaped
bodies of tropical parasites, the people that scan
the skies for rain and omen birds, the fear of avian flu.

Rainy Day

after Gustave Caillebotte, 1877

No, I haven't been to those streets
the caption says intersect near the Gare Saint-Lazare,
where gentlemen and ladies step out into the falling rain.
They stroll down a boulevard at the end of which rises
a brand-new building— Geometric in pearlescent light,
it houses what I imagine to be modern apartments,
a first-floor row of burgeoning cafés, flower shops,
patisseries, confectionery and milliners' stores. In one,
the couple in the painting's foreground might have purchased
cuff links for him, some eau de cologne, even the short-brimmed
bonnet she wears with its discreet mesh veil shading her eyes.

Rain being what it is, rain falls all day today as well in the south,
not south of Paris but through the Blue Ridge mountains,
over the Chesapeake, in the bible belt— where mildewed cornfields,
vehicles stalled in flash floods, a child's bright green
umbrella with frog eyes snagged in a bush, might suggest divine
retribution. The deluge, once more undoing the constructed world.

And so I admire the way rain sometimes looks decorous; how
pavement stones have the sheen of well-scrubbed oysters in *Paris Street:
Rainy Day.* Nothing suggests the more familiar pell-mell scrambling
for any open doorway, awning, or bus stop. Somberly attired,
passersby walk seemingly without hurry, with restraint,
though the hems of their good wool trousers and skirts must be

waterlogged. After all, what could one do to avoid
what will fall of its own accord and as if without
mystery? Rain thins to drizzle beyond the kitchen window;
the world outside looks strangely distant, like a place that could
forget you at any moment. In Caillebotte, even the brittle
ribs and paneled seams of silk umbrellas sigh in the rain
just a little; and, unless you look very close, the tiny
teardrop sheen of the woman's earring is hardly even there.

The Minim

In a music studio waiting room, waiting
for my daughter to emerge from piano lessons,

I read a magazine article on tubercular
Modigliani— how after his death, his lover Jeanne

leaped to her own from a Paris rooftop, pregnant
with his second child. It was a time

that critics describe as the emergence of
Modernity, the coming-of-age of that inconsolable

and perturbing child who gazes
through window gratings of an apartment

and sees the world fracturing into little cubes of blue.
What a world to have lived in, to have arrived in,

especially for the wayfarer, the exile
with his *portmanteau* of souvenirs, describing

the pavement between the world of no return and the world
of always beginning, and the light that shimmers

somewhere in the dusty trees. A public outcry shut down
his first exhibit, *because it threatened prevailing notions of decency—*

those women's necks lengthening in twilight, their tulip thighs
promising welcome. Not sixty years before,

the painters from Manila made their way to Rome and Barcelona.
Only fifth or sixth class, said Retana of Juan Luna; *no notable place*

among the ranks of Spanish painters. Reviewers said the same
of José Garcia Villa when he came to America to write

among the early Moderns: *at best, a minor poet.*
Modernity, Modernity, how cruel you've been

as Muse, demanding constant servitude and reinvention.
In Luna's *Spoliarium,* the two gladiators dragged from

the arena to the chamber of bodies where they will be
stripped and burned, leave rust-colored tracks upon the floor.

The music teacher, a Russian émigré
who used to be a biophysicist in her former life,

might recognize the paradox: distance
infinitely halved, never sutured close.

Spoliarium is a mural by Filipino painter Juan Luna (1857–1899). He was among the cohort of Filipino artists and scholars who went to Europe in the 1800s, where they pondered the problems arising from a corrupt colonial dispensation in the islands, the issues of cultural and linguistic identity, social reform, and a burgeoning Filipino nationalism. Luna entered *Spoliarium* in the Exposicion Nacional de Bellas Artes in 1884, where it won one of two gold medals. In 1886 it was sold for 20,000 pesetas. It currently hangs in the National Musuem of the Philippines.

DECODING THE SIGNATURE

Kept towns,
attached, still we knew
to follow. Yearning
allows knowledge. Thunder,
yew tree leaning dangerous
on the cliff face—

How many names
for desert winds?
Imagine that historian
swallowed in a column of sand
so he could learn
even a few
of its hundred forms:

Whirling *djinn,*
copper fire.
Rifi. Ghibli.
Harmattan. Solano.
The stop in the breath
from knowing
inside the name.

Alloys keep their yes;
they've married
or intermingled
in the fat of gold.
They should never
be poor again,
if not for heat.

Who will read
and by what light, fallen
like stars years from now,
figures on the stone
fresco?

All parts of the body
ready for the other,
the atoms of desire
deflecting, one
moment more,

ready to forgive
the curve of distance,
the hunger that follows.

In the Clothing Archive

*Barong Tagalog**

How cold the world grows.
          Under a moon dyed the colors of rust
               and blood, threads spin

out of the bodies of worms.
          The pith of green stalks feeds
               old fires. I embroider

suspicion with my hands. Worn
          loose, ends untucked, it declares
               there is nothing I conceal.

Rendered so, I am a field
          open always to diminishment.
               I am the skull

under extensions of flesh,
          the smile of a blade,
               an amulet of nicked

---

* The *Barong Tagalog* is a traditional Filipino men's shirt of sheer piña (pineapple) or jusi fabric, decorated by hand with intricate embroidery. Spanish colonial authorities were said to have enforced the costume in order to ensure that male colonial subjects were not concealing weapons on their persons.

bone. Wear it and wed
        me, invisible shroud, my pale other. History
                decorated with disappearing

stars and lacunae, it's why
        you want to look
                even as you avert your gaze.

Letras y Figuras

This art genre . . . began with albums of commissioned paintings by colonial officials and wealthy traders from the West who wanted to show images of the exotic peoples and places they had traveled, to their compatriots back home.

— Alfredo Roces, *Adios, Patria Adorada*

The security guard at the Museum explains
that the ochre discoloration at the bottom

of a pair of waist-high, gold-brushed
Chinese jars, might be because of the remote

location of public restrooms on that floor.
Every relic bears a scar, then— the arts

in 17th century *Filipinas,* like a new *bahay
na bato* at the end of a row of wooden houses,

waiting to be filled with *tipos del pais,*
paintings as virtual albums of island life:

a farmer stands all day ankle-deep in water,
diligent at the sod; a native woman kneels

to graze with her lips the hand of the bishop.
Indifferently he walks in the street. A young boy follows,

bearing on a silk pillow what I see now
is a red and gold *biretta* and not, as I first thought,

the pullet that lays the bishop's breakfast— eggs
he likes to eat with buttered *ensaimada* and thick

chocoláte. In Marché's *La rue de l'Escolta
á Manille*, 1886, the church is the point before

the vanishing point, its spire drawn high
against the scattering clouds— the obvious sermon

from which all figures in the foreground have for the moment
turned. The noodle-seller sets down his pole and baskets;

the women balancing clay jars on their heads
pause to wipe their hands on their *camisas.*

Two late risers slide an upstairs window open,
and the driver of the *caruaje* swivels his head

to look in the painter's direction— and in mine,
anonymous face returning to these frames, curious about

the watery skies and ivory light, about Giraudier's
El Escribiente, 1860, and what has made him push back his chair

from the lace-covered table to read so intently; why he stands
and bows his head, as if in prayer, over such a small scrap of paper.

Art works referenced in the poem:

    El Escribiente, by lithographer Baltasar Giraudier, *Ilustracion Filipina*, July 1, 1860.

    La rue de l'Escolta á Manille, colored print by Alfred Marche, 1886. Marche was a French explorer and collector of ethnographic, anthropological, and zoological objects, who had also visited West Africa. He made two voyages to the Philippines (1879–1881 and 1883–1885), and wrote *Voyage Aux Philippines*.

    Native Woman Greeting a Priest, by Jose Honorato Lozano, in *Album: Islas Filipinas, 1663–1888*, Jose Maria A. Carino and Sonia Pinto Ner (Makati City, Philippines: Ars Mundi, Philippinae, 2004).

The art genre known as *tipos del pais* began when colonial officials and wealthy foreign traders in the Philippines commissioned albums of paintings in order to show images of the exotic people and places they had encountered in their travels. The earliest example of *tipos del pais* is known as *The Boxer Codex* (c. 1595). The most famous artist of the *tipos del pais* genre was Jose Honorato Lozano, who in the mid-1800s developed a style of embellishing letters of the alphabet (as illuminated medieval manuscripts were wont to do) with *tipos del pais* scenes and imagery; this latter subgenre came to be known as "Letras y Figuras."

Bahay na bato (Tagalog): stone house.

JUAN LUNA'S REVOLVER

could well be the subtitle of an opera
        performed to a mostly well-heeled crowd
                in Manila's National Museum

— among the audience, the great-grandniece
        of the famous painter's murdered wife.
                The latter's name was Paz (meaning peace,

that dream of living without fear of arousing
        violence when confronted by the strange or
                uncanny, or that which seems to bear

little resemblance to ourselves). Looking
        at pictures of compatriots
                abroad in the nineteenth century, why

should we think everything was profiteroles,
        white gloves, silk ties, salon conversation,
                bellas artes? Bumping into the Filipino,

a woman on the streets of Madrid regards
        his Malay features and exclaims, *But how well*
                you speak Spanish (lo posea tanto como yo)!

It's said the painter's *mestiza* wife
        and mother-in-law paid for more than half
                the rent of his studio and apartments.

Yet one September in Paris, in 1892,
        he barged into the bedroom
                and shot them both: his wife, on suspicion of

an amorous liaison with a Frenchman
        (possibly taller, possibly better endowed,
                though he himself was said to have wondered

how it could be, given that Paz was *not*
        especially attractive); his mother-
                in-law, her brains marbling the mantel,

because she valiantly tried to stop him.
        All accounts thereafter become the Petri
                dish for gossip: his trial in a French court,

his conviction of *nothing more*
        than a crime of passion. His return to
                the motherland after seventeen years;

his arrest and pardon for alleged
        complicity in the revolution
                against Spain. The desultory

paintings after, that critics say never again
        approach the scale of that mural the world
                admired in Barcelona: a pair of bodies,

bloodied and dragged through Roman columns
  from the arena. Searching the internet for more
    on Paz and her mother, I stumble on

news reports of one other Juan Luna,
  Mexican-born *family man* who grew up
    in Palatine, Illinois: with his

high school friend he burst into Brown's Chicken
  one January day in 1993,
    killing everyone they found there.

They fled, perhaps spent the night in the woods
  where small creatures scrape their limbs together
    to make this sound that often passes for music.

Juan Luna the painter was pardoned
  and ordered to pay one franc each
    to his victims' immediate relatives,

because of an obscure French law which explained
  that native people, very primitive people,
    have this tendency to run amok.

LUCES

Ilustrados, the "Enlightened ones"

> ... though one may look and sound foreign, underneath one is in control of one's
> identity. In effect taking vengeance is simultaneous with putting the foreign in its
> "proper" place: outside of oneself, a mere disguise and thus an instrument with
> which to carry out one's will.
>
> — Vicente L. Rafael, *The Promise of the Foreign*

From a yellow room overlooking a brick courtyard
damp from yesterday's rain, I glance at a pair of ducks

sculpted in stone. My thoughts turn to *paté
de foie gras* not from hunger, but because

I have been reading about the Malolos Convention
of 1899, of how, at the banquet to inaugurate

the first Philippine Republic, gold-tasseled
menus were written in French and the food

was foreign: *Saumon Hollandais, Coquilles
de Crabes, Jambon Froid, Cotelettes de Mouton*

a la Papillote. . . . Foreign, that is, to the native
palate— even that cuisine described as

Cocido Filipino, an archive of the tongue's journeys
outside its original home.

But doesn't departure carry
the possibility of return? I read in another article

that *sardinas secas,* a kind of dried and salted fish
the poor can afford to eat, was the favorite breakfast

of the great hero Rizal. Not *pan y chocoláte,*
not eggs fried or scrambled, even if

they could recently begin to serve *mantequilla*
in creamy yellow molds because ice had found

its way to the colony: mini glaciers packed in straw,
traveling to the tropics in the hold of a ship

which also carried gramophones, painted tiles
and gold-rimmed crystal from Strasbourg and Austria.

Imagine fair *mestizas* dancing the waltz
after supper, the young men

recently returned from Europe. Castilian in dress
and manners, but also something else—

Fathered by friars and farmers' wives,
by scholars, merchants, and

revolutionaries, a new invention. These bodies
that bore the idea of nation, *los indios bravos.*

AUIT / SONG

Sa loob at labas ng bayan cong saui
Kaliluha'i siyang nangyayaring Hari.

Within and without my hapless country
Tyranny has come to reign.
— Francisco Balagtas, *Florante at Laura*

Today she walks a tended path in the prairie,
the surviving forest held in check at its edges.
Someone has stacked dead wood and broken shingles
in the open space where bonfires burned each year

for a century. Prints of passing animals,
furtive signs of life in the margins— what nature
or habit of mind returns to that which is
not present? On summer's eves, this lawn

might have played host to scenes from alien histories:
that verse play in Tagalog, where abandoned prince
Florante laments his fate in the woods, unabashed
cries heard by the banished moor Aladdin.

Sharing their common narratives— betrayal and desire
turning fathers into lovers and murderers,
kingdoms recently reduced to panic and rubble—
they recognize each other in their suffering.

She imagines their mixed idioms in the wilderness
turning enmity into love and pity; imagines
rain in cities falling on the beheaded, the loud
static of crickets, scoring and scoring the nights.

The *auit* or *awit* (song) was a verse form in vernacular Tagalog. In the original form, the *auit* typically consisted of four rhyming *aaaa* lines per stanza, with each line having around twelve syllables, and many figures of speech. One of the most famous *auits* is Francisco Balagtas' 339-stanza *Florante at Laura* (1861).

DOCTRINA CHRISTIANA

The good colonial tends to his lessons in the new tongue daily,
but when he writes prayers in Spanish, they are not his first *versos* in history.

Aloft on a pulley, dark hair set with roses, the announcing angel on Easter
    morning
sings *"Regina Coeli, Laetare!"* above a church nave, as though lifted from history.

When the Passion of Christ was translated, the first important revelation
for natives was that a peon— a carpenter— was the son of the God of history.

During Lent, elders chant the *Cinaculo* on their knees. Ululating voices mourn
outlawed epics full of savage life, of deities' cloud-layers, of heroes' amazing
    histories.

The *Moro-moro* and *Komedya* were verse plays in vernacular, wild with paste-
    paper costumes
and epic battles between Christian and Moorish kingdoms in medieval Europe's
    history.

Muslim vendors, migrants from the Philippine south, spread vials of perfume
on embroidered robes, poised to run from authorities as they've done through-
    out history.

My mothers sit at a table spread with comfrey, snipping hearts from their stalks,
to strain a tonic for ailments known to women chastened by history.

Here are the points against which I align my sense of destination:
duty and longing, twin bulbs that flicker in the long-playing marquee of history.

In the old plays, *Principe* Constantino must win a *torneo* for his Florencia.
Once in a while, a glimpse of her face, her story, beneath history.

Once in a while, traces of a palimpsest beneath parables and aphorisms
that filled my childhood with conflicting counsel: valor and piety; or, waiting
 makes history.

So names are never innocent— miniature manuscripts, illuminated with the
 wishes of those who gave them.
For mine, *Maria Luisa,* either a martyr's or warrior's, what were they thinking
 was to be my history?

Cinaculo: passion play, or the life, passion and death of Jesus Christ, chanted and often enacted
as religious drama during Lent, and said to have been introduced by Spanish clergy in the
Philippines to supplant indigenous (pagan) epics.

Mil Besos

In this town filled with solid Midwestern architecture
    and the barely noticeable twang of vowels, she is unsure

of why ghosts of foreign languages haunt her,
    even those she has not learned enough to master.

She copies phrases from books she reads— *lenguaje electrico,*
    lenguaje del rayo— intuiting their patina, tasting their

elusive salt. Her daughter, sleepy from waitressing
    at a Japanese restaurant, yawns on the phone.

She laughs and says *Good night, eat something*;
    there are ghosts everywhere. Here among sweet clover,

coneflowers, queen anne's lace, and other respectable weeds,
    she feels monkish, brown. Her brother-in-law remarks

at lunch that hazelnut butter is *So Euro.* Years ago,
    her Castilian grandmother fell and shattered

her pelvis on the patio. Bedridden three years before her death,
    she darkened in the sheets like a mildewed El Greco.

Punctually after midnight, the plaintive command: *ven aqui!*
    which her son's wife met with bedpan and warm water.

Light dapples the windows in a room where linens
    and sheets have just been changed. There is no smell

of lavender water, but she remembers how she and her mother
would climb the seventy-five steps to the Cathedral.

During Lent, candle wax petaled the mosaic floors.
Penitents bowed to kiss the statue of the crucified Christ

laid prone on a velvet bier— in each painted wound, the trace
of spittle flowering from fervent, uncountable mouths.

Black Elk in Paris

Paris Universal Exposition, 1889

— para los Indios bravos

Today's *Chicago Tribune* has a picture,
a trio of new wax statues at Madame Tussaud's:

lifelike but vague in flannel, the infant Shiloh
and her famous parents lately involved in philanthropy.

Brad slouches behind Angelina in a baseball cap.
She's clad in t-shirt and denim jeans, the bow of her

famous pout mirroring the shape of a necklace
against her collarbone, a single strand of cowrie shells

corded on leather. Such trinkets
might have been the wampum Buffalo Bill Cody

made his Indians thread— Sitting Bull,
Chief Joseph, Geronimo, Black Elk,

even Rains-in-the-Face (reputed to be
the man who killed Custer), Ghost Dancers

made to choose between prison
or joining the Wild West Show.

In that carnival standing in for the dusty frontier,
Rizal and his friends admired

staged battles and skirmishes, war paint
and feathered regalia. *Why should we resent*

being called Indios by the Spaniards?
Look at those Indios from North America . . .

Let us be like them. We shall be Indios Bravos!
It's said that Black Elk, an Oglala Sioux,

had traveled to London to meet Queen Victoria.
He missed the boat taking the Wild West Show

back to America, but found work with other
traveling exhibitions. Who knows now why every

popular museum and cigar shop has a painted
Indian, or why we like to put shiny copper pennies

in a machine to press them long and flat,
like arrowheads? Who knew that a year later,

a hundred and forty-six *Indios* would die
defending Wounded Knee, or that far away in the east,

other *Indios* were plotting a revolution,
signing their names in their own real blood.

II /

THE CLEAR BONES

The Clear Bones

Some say bone was the first kind of paper,
difficult to inscribe because it involved fractures
or accidents. Vellum and parchment came later,
then linen, canvas, reams of book paper. Lifted whole

from the dark ocean bed, a ribcage is an archive.
All the gaps between, the missing years that must be
filled in by hand: at an archaeologist's pit or artist's
easel; under laboratory lights or the glow cast by

a tasseled lamp over a séance table. Divination
is the art of reading the future, which is the blue
horizon dissolving like tissue in the distance,
or the level bars that make up a rune in the I Ching.

Early soothsayers threw dice made of astragali—
heel bones of hooved animals like antelope or sheep,
filed down and squared to fit the palm of the hand.
Think of the almond rattling, a little bone sheathed

in its case; a pair of plastic dice rolling onto the flocked
nap of a table, announcing their mystical numerals.
Think of the bookmaker's *baren* dried from
cuttlebone, burnishing the spine that promises,

in time, to crack fully open. Mother, every day is still
a gift or curse. The bones steep in salt and water, water
and salt and air. I've tasted mouths and tongues and skins
of salt and yet I am no closer to divining their meaning

than the day you called the old bonesetter and her sister
to prophesy. Dressed in the colors and smells of old
tobacco, they lit candles in our living room and scared
the bejesus out of me. They flicked dry nails across

the riverbeds of my palms, crooning as if to someone
already drowned. I'd wanted to go away to the mountains
with a man nine years older, and there sketch pictures
of deer, bats lining the mummy caves, a mountain lake

hidden in blankets of fog. Perhaps I died anyway or perished
in flames I did not smell nor see burning, when I made my way.
Perhaps I floated across a river of warnings into the afterworld,
only to be returned for my desires. Everything I want is still

at arm's length, a current of blue swirling with
the hint of silver. Shackle and oar, what stains the water?
Nomad, I move from one address to another, pack and carry
my worldly belongings only to unpack them in strange,

new rooms. I'm hurtled back to the beginning. Some nights
the dove of sleep lays its own head on its indigo breast
and cries for release. O Mother, the dream remains,
like window bars, like vertebrae in beveled chains.

SEDIMENT

Connoisseur has a hidden undertone
like spice, the very last thread of scent
secreted in a hard knob

of purest cassia cinnamon, though the jar
has long been empty. The nose
remembers what childhood was like—

a village of camphor bottles, the sting
of pine needles raining on a lake
in summer. Some days hard

sun on tar reminds her of burnt
sugar, heat pooling into shapes
by which to tell the hours,

the heart's conditions: star anise,
comfrey, pu-erh, jasmine, oolong,
pointed-leaf-jade, green peony—

a line of empty tins on a shelf promising
sleep, wakefulness, release; the clarity
to see as stone, as water.

Riddle

Sa araw ay bungbong
Sa gabi ay dagat

A reed that leans against the wall in the morning
becomes the sea at night
         — *Salawikain* / Philippine proverb

We moved into the apartment in summer, the top
floor of a house built in the 1900s— cathedral

ceilings, a nonworking fireplace with carved moldings
(pineapple crowns and fans, because this is the south),

wood floors that I buff every so often with
half a coconut husk. Two bedrooms open

through French doors onto a sleeping porch.
Broken screens let in mosquitoes so they hover

on the outer lips of our ears, looking for
the trickster that stole fire from their caves,

the flower whose beacon blazed in the night.
I put my youngest child to bed with legends

I was told as a girl. She giggles at the sound
of foreign consonants and brushes her long hair out

upon the pillow, wondering why it isn't yellow.
In the morning her bangle rolls under the table,

and that's when we see the rusty buzzer
inlaid in the middle of the dining room floor.

My neighbor says it must have been
used by the master and mistress of the house

to summon servants from below. Up
and down the narrow basement steps,

bringing tea in frosted glasses,
laundry from the hamper, a baby

unlatched from the wet nurse's breast.
Insistent messenger at my ear, unroll

your pallet and go to sleep. The sounds of silver
chafe in the kitchen. The shapes of china

harp in the cupboards, crack and crackle like the sea.

— *for Mary Cornish*

Bypass

Vancouver, British Columbia

A scar in the middle of her chest
just below the collarbone, shaped like
the body of a dragonfly. The pucker

where stitches used to be, uneven
lines radiating to form the shadow
of wings. She shuffles to the kitchen

to pour oil into a pan, moistens the day-
old rice, pauses for a breath. A freezer
magnet holds the photo of her husband,

dead eight years, buoyed by tiny
plastic roses. She gestures at the backyard
that will need seeding, the marks along the ceiling

of this new house where her son will lay
decorative molding. A great room, foyer, den,
plus two rooms on each floor. She fixes it

so like all the houses she has owned (four)
and sold (three), downstairs there are separate
apartments— mortgage helpers. She's taken in

only those moving between worlds:
house painters waiting for their papers,
women who cannot return to wherever it was

they left in a hurry. Yesterday at the harbor front
the loudmouth selling bottles of metal polish
singles her out for the awkwardness of her tongue.

She steers me away saying, *It's not true,*
Surrey's no more crime-infested than the city. They dump
the bodies in our neighborhoods, then blame foreign scum.

The water slides under the ferry like a plate
of milk. A woman with a knapsack turns to smile
before her brown face disappears into the crowd.

BARTER

Salt, island light, distant
    ribbon of sea always a mirage—

        Iron roofs along the edge of the viewfinder,
          then the coast—

Count the knobs on splayed toes
    the stiff fringe bordering loincloths

      Three Chinese jars, raw ore from the hills,
        a side of smoked venison

        I'll wager the child with the herringbone tattoo
          wonders about taste

Molasses hardened in half a coconut shell
    Corn and dried salt fish

Sacks of red grain
    Round scallop shells polished in brine

      Your shield for a water buffalo
        Your heirloom beads for a plastic rosary

Bitter gourds sharpen the tongue
    A padlock claps its grin on the earlobe

        How many heads for a funeral blanket

Antique, all-organic vegetable dyes,
    one hundred percent cotton
        pulled taut on a backstrap loom

Ten Thousand Villages

Five dry gourds to make a musical rattle like water
cascading over stones. Purses made from wealth
discarded by llamas stepping through trails
lined with prickly vines. Soap from the neem tree,
fragrance from slippery skins of overripe mangos
stirred in metal vats. Women set them to heat on fires
crackling to life outside a circle of huts. The rainbow
folds of a *serape* next to last season's newspapers,
each page torn and coiled and dipped in glue to make
a set of placemats. My children wander through aisles
almost narrow as jungle paths, patting *papier mache*
elephants pedicured with paisley, nativity scenes small
miracles of cornhusk and dimpled grain. All this
jeweled wealth (*oh pretty!*) made from strings and red clay,
from castoff skins, from blue-green bottoms of cola
bottles, broken into necklaces of raw silver.
Purchase a basket and clothe a child.
A teakwood cabinet with no nails might feed
a mountain community for a month. *How wonderful,*
exclaims a customer, admiring a *salwar kameez*
dyed the colors of the lipstick tree. Part of her forty
dollars will travel across the world and take up the hands
of weaver girls so patiently knotting threads as though
they awaited bridegrooms, tell them their industry has not
been in vain. Fingering transparent domes of food
covers embroidered with colored straw, I remember the year
my whole elementary school raked vegetable plots
behind the convent— Afternoons, in place of PE

or home economics, we turned the soil with makeshift trowels,
scattered seeds and squealed at the slime of earthworms.
For trellises, we drove overlapping stakes into the ground.
For watering cans, we took empty cans of soup
or fruit cocktail and punched holes along the bottom.
When the school year ended, we cheered as pale blue
sweet pea flowers emerged, and the firm jade ovals of tomatoes;
but never paused to wonder who picked them in the summertime,
who boiled pots of conserve or decorated bowls of salad—
all the red we had grown with our hands.

IRREVERSIBLES

1

And then there was light —
light to fill the skull and its bones
with the matter of flesh and leaves.
I walked in a Zen garden once— spring
rain, spirals pearling in gravel. Everything
so still: whorls of cypress against a doll-
house hut, bamboo dipper open like a hand
beside a barrel of water. I wanted to lie
under the sill, to catch the receding
hours along my forearm, the precise
texture of darkness when it fell.

2

Cave walls adorned with picture writing.
The smear of pigments on rice powder.
You spoke of *horror vacuii,* that fear of the void
meant to explain the elaborate gesture, the surplus.
You said, *think of the celtic knot, each complicated
loop within a loop,* as your fingers stroked
the lips of my labia open.

3

A dictator had ordered likenesses
of himself and his wife painted
as angels on the walls of a basilica—
the mural by the altar with its
quartz blues and siennas.
Tourists drink the holy
water, speculating on life
after life. Cobbled streets
echo every inquisitive footfall.
You could walk to the market
for bags of local sausages and fried
cured pork in oily parchment, dunk
churros in *chocoláte* in the shadow of
a bell tower. When heat has pooled
in the high windows, every surface
is a slate filled with scallops.

4

What of the barely even seen?
The way light passes continually,
as though rinsing to color the glass.
The way I fall back or pull away
from this body's need to see and touch
another that isn't merely its reflection,
to break the spell of its own randomness.

MISSION REPORT

Ignorance is a treasure of infinite price.
                    — Paul Valery

You write of your week in southern Sudan,
the Russian plane landing on a muddy airstrip
three days' hike from any village.

A column of mosquitoes escorts you at dusk
to the camp where your group is not yet expected.
This partly explains the tarpaulin tents and makeshift

bathroom, the plastic basin, the jerrican of water.
A villager motions welcome, sifting tablespoons
of Tang into a pitcher of brown water.

Because all eyes are watching, you drink
from the plastic tumbler and peel boiled cassava
with your fingers. The drone of a bottlefly

leads to the latrine, a pit barely screened
by horse grass. Near dawn, the panicked
sounds of nearby gunfire, then the night guard's

confession at breakfast: he'd fired
his Kalashnikov rifle at a hyena attempting to devour
a cow in the field. This is the same man who laughs

at the idea— to build a raft, perhaps in time,
a series of footbridges across the river to towns
where one might get matches, kerosene, candles,

soap, medicine. He shakes his head: *no bambu here,*
bambu the only wood will float. No one blinks when a Black
Mamba slithers out from under your mattress,

but when you go from hut to hut asking to borrow
rope and machetes, they think you are crazy as the hyena
with the big mouth. For days you hack at saplings

and lash them to each other. Single-handed, you drag and push
the thing into the shallows, but when it bobs then floats
downstream, they all cheer. *I can build many,*

the night guard promises. Someone brings more Tang
to celebrate. There hasn't been a gurgle of complaint
from your stomach: a miracle, deep in the bush like this.

Interregnum

. . . shade I am doomed to follow,
my perfect double.
— Billy Collins

In a dream she thinks she has fallen
into, a party's in progress. Music
touches the drapes and the greenery,

the fluted glasses that hold their one
clear note of wine. The table spreads
in all directions like an orchard

ripe with fruit. Reaching to partake
of the feast, she's served what barely
grazes the throat with sweetness:

small portions, glazed
marzipans to be nibbled
politely, morsels that accuse

with their aftertaste of past failures.
She does not really care for such food
dispensed in the awkwardness

of smiling and chatting with people
she knows but can never remember
her name. There's a circle of bodies pressed

close like flowers in the middle of the room.
Perhaps the host or hostess is serving coffee
and secrets. She tries to make her way,

but that's when Death comes through the door
in the guise of a valet parking attendant. Hat dusted
with snow, holding out car keys, his worn overcoat's

much too long and the ends sweep the floor. She knows
he's only a messenger, but because she's been taught
that obedience is virtue, she foresees how

she will follow him out almost by instinct,
will climb into the vehicle waiting to take her away. But
any moment now the foliage will stipple, the leaves detach from

darkness. She considers what would happen
if he tripped, if she pinned down the tails of his coat
with her heel. She hears an owl cry silver,

the moon's tapestry needle clattering out of the sky.

Archipelago

The scent of camphor strays across a hedge
    and I am back on Mabini, where as a child

I stared at man-roots growing filaments, fluid-filled mason jars
    next to powders ground from deer horn and dried seahorses.

It wasn't till later that I'd read of revolutionaries
    and blood compacts, an island traded for a hat,

the annual parade of caravelles and galleons
    setting sail for Spanish ports, their holds filled

with copra and anise, barrels steeped with stolen
    fragrances, bales of peppercorn and laurel. The dead

swim back and forth alongside these vessels, brown-skinned
    sailors and their sad Marias, throwing cameos

on black ribbons at the moon. The dead,
    not Magellan, circumnavigate the world,

jump ship somewhere near Louisiana, build houses
    on stilts. The dead are magnetized by the call of water.

The dead peer through bedroom curtains, including
    Grandmother, half-breed who wants to tame

your tongue and braid your *india* hair tighter than
    that careless peasant bun. *Infidel, will you return to the house*

that holds the ghosts of your forbears? I'll look for the town of Zafra,
    I'll look for the villages of San Fernando and San Juan,

for a yellow house where the statue of San Vicente
    sits at the foot of *El Sagrado Corazon,* his blood

perfumed with roses. I'll close my eyes and imagine
    ceilings fed with rain, where every night

mold-stippled constellations emerge, islands too
    insignificant for any maps save those in our vagabond hearts.

... little, wooly headed, black, dwarf savages ...
not far above the anthropoid apes ... a link which is not missing
but soon will be.

— Dean C. Worcester

III /

THE ARROWS FIT EXACTLY INTO THE WOUNDS*

---

*attributed to Kafka

Ekphrasis

Chrysler Museum

At the museum fronting the Hague
        a stallion rears up on its hind legs because
the bridle that is history's wants it to stay
        its previous course— At least that's how

it might be read: the figure seated on the horse,
        torqued from its axis; the other wounded, lifting
an arm, a head, from dust. Because the animal's
        hooves are raised, it seems a sound

has rattled the pavement, a pair of chariot-wheels
        startled the random traffic of geese under the bridge.
I walk sometimes by water to watch light touch
        trees, pillars, roofs briefly with gold.

Where we first met in rooms hung with tapestry,
        with pictures narrating saints' lives and martyrdoms,
orbs of blown Venetian glass swung low. Giant stars
        ticked above display cases where swords arched in rows

next to their mated sheaths. O evidence of plated
        armor, o silk of embroidered robes— what is the catalogue
of your shedding? Only a moment, sensed more
        than seen: the soul at the boundary of passage.

Lyrica Obscura

I no longer believe
in the objective world,
the one the camera
and critics call *realistic.*

I look at a painting
of a house with awnings
somewhere in Florida,
and the elusiveness of memory

is the aperture I fall through.
Where am I now? Not in Key West
where I have never been, but
walking to the end of the road and

into the next street where, for a time,
mother bought bread and meat
from the wives of rabbit farmers.
We tore into the yeasty heart

as she hummed in the kitchen,
sharpening her knife.
Our noses twitched.
The walls were silky with ears.

WANTING

The birdcage is the work
I am after: gold-barred,
so no bird leaves.
　　　— Rick Barot, "Miro's Notebook"

A table by an open window,
dogwood, magnolia.

The mind's interruptions
of memory: flame trees,

bread wrapped in crackling
brown paper, carol of absent

roosters. Shaken loose, willow trees
trouble the lake's surface. Heat

will undo the exactitude
of doorways, wrap summer fruit

with a white mantle
akin to frost. I dream

of flowers erupting without
cease upon the green tendril

and its arc, unable to contain
their solitude.

PROVISIONAL

Where are you standing? A ledge,
I said; will you meet for coffee at ten?
The view around my feet is carpet, gray,
lackluster. I'm reading a poem,
meant to be recited to *sabar* or *gangsa.*
I'd recognize their sound. Memories come
to me like the afternoon I heard two cats in heat
on the roof of our old house. Did I tell you
of the time I walked in circles around Edinburgh?
I've always had some place to which I thought
I could return. Still not gypsy enough,
but I spread my towel on the pitched roof and lay there,
a lizard, not moving, my heart pounding.
I love the sun in any form. I saw
hills, shadows of slow-moving sheep, static
wildflowers. At the castle
where I slept and wrote three weeks,
we glimpsed a woman and a child in bright
clothing, twigs in their hair, all mismatched
tartan. They lit a fire at the edge of the wood.
The river was called Esk.
Someone on the castle property saw and threatened
their trespass with a rifle. I am not joking.
In another life a man said to me *Give up*
your writing. Then all will be happy or else. You see
I haven't stopped. I have children.

You've seen the stretch marks.
So, you said, next to my cheek your shoulder
nearly as brown as my own,
How long since you tasted yourself?
Here we are. We drink steaming coffee,
mine with a little milk.
We smile and talk, barely even touching.

THE KITCHEN GIRL'S JOURNAL

To live a life, that it might be written—
that it might be lifted, whole

as a tin pail brimful with water, blue
as cyanotype from inverted bowls

of spoons lying on the drainboard.
In the age of *belles lettres,* I imagine the random

musings of even an ordinary journal-keeper
to have been such careful compositions:

living in a time when the nib of a pen
sliding across a creamy surface was still

for the most part a new invention, with what
slow pleasure I know I would count,

when I could, the bright abacus of the also
recently discovered hours. I would loosen

my apron-strings and finger the bound
signatures, nose out the faint watermark

(the grassy smell of their drying
in the sun, pressed into each rectangle).

Pots of common herbs on the sill
tell of names from a dreamer's

catalogue: field cabbage, black mustard,
Chinese parsley, *kinchay* and *yerba buena,*

bristly ox tongue, nipplewort.
Between the doorknob and the handle

of the broom, the gill and belly of
a gutted milkfish; between the trussed

pairs of quail, small cavities I will line
with bay leaf and wild rice. Here

I'll steal an hour— where my finger,
turning a page, can trace deckled edges,

torn heads of marsh marigold, twists
of knotgrass picked on a solitary walk.

La Americana

Reading about Rembrandt's restored
painting of a woman with a bonnet, I thought
of the girl who used to come and do odd jobs
around the neighborhood and in my
childhood home— laundry once a week
(hand-wash, line-dry, iron and fold), yard work,
a little dusting. My aunts explained, her mother
must have looked too often at the sun while she
was in the womb; how else did she acquire
those white-fringed brows and lashes, pale irises,
mottled skin, hair the color and texture of straw,
blond in a country of midnight hair and eyes?

I didn't know her real name, only that when
she walked past the corner store, men called
"*Puraw*" (almost like calling your dog
"Whitey"). Women were kinder, giving her
lunch, the care of little ones, while she waited
for their clothes to dry. "*Americana,*" they sang,
"who's your G.I. from the land of milk
and honey?" while wrapping leftovers
in newspaper for her and her mother.

Before the portrait's recent restoration, art
scholars had puzzled the discrepancy between
the rich fur collar and the plain starched linen
bonnet. The planes below the cheeks on this
unremarkable if solid-looking face, reflected
light from a hidden source until x-rays
revealed a collar of yellowed ivory: pressed
cotton, sturdy and clean enough to wear
to church— the kind that maids and serving
girls fastened over everyday frocks. I think
about both girls, the one in the portrait
and the other who could have served as well
as Rembrandt's model, about the little spot
of color along the cheekbones and the other
things that remain invisible, unnamed.

Koken's Barbershop

Session Road, Baguio City

The smell was always of talcum powder and pomade,
the smell of shaving cream and warm water

into which the barber with the bow tie shook
precisely six drops of lavender. He rubbed

the white nap of terrycloth on a service face towel
across customers' cheeks, chins. Their necks

lay open on the headrest, trusting the blade
to scrape hard stubble away in a sweep of foam.

Then, no women came here except
the manicurist, a girl with one blind eye

and the same pink cardigan worn day after day.
She rinsed towels in an enamel basin then bent

over each finger to file and buff their nails and lacquer
clear. Where they went afterward in their wool

and gabardine or pinstriped suits was of no
concern to her, nor that the barber's chairs each

came from a different factory— engraved metal plates
on trestles proclaiming *Ohio 1905,* or *Illinois 1910,*

their footrests covered with grime, the wine-colored
upholstery twice refurbished in a local shop.

Venom

In every bottle of Caballeros
triple-distilled mezcal, a scorpion

swims in a silo of liquid the color
of caramel, of clarified *dulce de leche,*

the hot milk of it pressed from a mulch
of chopped blue agave hearts, *maguey azul.*

Darker than an olive dropped into a martini,
it's there as a memento of what follows

after the flush of pleasure, after the heat
that turns the knees into a mush like *pulque*

because though she said she wouldn't allow it,
she's let her heart float to her mouth—

it lies on its side like a fish in cold
stupor and her tongue has gone numb

like a stone. All because she's fallen
for the one she can't have, she tosses

her head back and drains the little cups
like they were poison, remembering

the sting of lime on his tongue, the bite of salt
in the crevice between his finger and thumb.

AUIT / SONG

Sister, why do you sit in front with the driver?
The dead are to be followed by the living.
The living walk in procession behind the hearse.

When we were young we went barefoot and picked green plums
in the garden. Did you wish to be the first one across?
But only I ventured to slip ripe skin with my teeth.

Often, you punished me. I bore my secret name
in silence. The rooms in your house are filled with cloth.
Don't you hear a silver lure singing in darkness,

somewhere just out of reach?

Meridian

Not the palm tree on left, nor the puddle
of shadow under the mail truck with its
insignia of wings. Not the tri-

colored tips of the bird-of-paradise plant
or the bougainvillea vines next to the fence,
nor even the adobe walls in signature

flamingo. What remains is this light,
delivering its first and only letter—
who lives here is no longer

here, who once struck blind
the ivory keys behind a curtain—
practicing, practicing—

one day felt the dead
weight of the familiar.
This is what it really means

when they say that sometimes,
a kind of halo encircles the ordinary:
the seal around windows can, after all,

be broken. Heat rises above
the town and its landmarks, dispersing
over a wilderness of directions.

WORTH

What is to be worthy or un-
worthy of another? *If there*
is fever, there is also work,
a woman wrote in a book
I read. She recollected
a story and the gift
of an apple to a famous painter:
he set it down on a tabletop
and looked at it for days,
the way its red burned
wilder than a berry or the feathers
on a bird of spring.
Against the window or yet again
arranged beside a yellow handful
of lemons, and still he would not touch
nor eat. Is this then a parable
about virtue, how at the end of suffering
there is the consolation of art?
Cixous says she prefers another method—
to bite into the fruit and open her mouth
to its compact cache of sweetness—
by which I am made to understand desire
inherits more desire, this work
of building memory of apple back by seed,
flower, spiral, when not even its core
remains. How could one forget?
The eye cleaves harder to any picture
shaded with the ink of loss.

Marine Layer

In Bergman's "Autumn Sonata"
      the leaves in the orchard have deepened
            to russet and brown. In the distance,

a train pulls away into the mountains
      as notes from a Chopin etude
            descend from the trees

to make a dressing gown for the mother.
      My head inclines toward the music as if I
            were the one being instructed on restraint

in the matter of sorrow— But how could it ever
      be possible to mute the sounds of breaking,
            the sounds a daughter makes, falling?

How can the listener only hover at the door frame
      doing nothing, like a moth hopelessly fluttering its wings?
            The women gesture and cry in the beautiful room.

The fire dies down in the parlor and the lover packs his bags
      for a solitary destination. Incommensurate, yes,
            though not at all inconceivable.

In the film, as in real life, the sea remains— its salt tang
      mixed with the odors of jasmine and gardenia,
            its surface lanced with light and scrolling

from page to page without cease. Climbing up the coast,
      crossing the bridge, it is what you hear even before emerging
            from the fog, dark-layered and measured as octaves.

DOLOROSA

after Michelangelo Merisi da Caravaggio's "Death of the Virgin"
(c. 1601–1603)

Death may have taken its time coming,
lending a slip of pallor to the clay, idling
among the stones and furrows in the orchard,

wringing the towel with the body's water
and effluvia into the pewter basin— It's still here,
in this room where the light tenders its departure,

a weight that causes Magdalen to double over.
Her coiled braids make me want to sob, her dress
the moldering tint of peaches in summer, her nape

caught in the last rays of sun falling from a high window.
Grown men with balding pates and pilgrims' beards
stand under a canopy, leathered red muted with sienna,

that Caravaggio paints as an inverted triangle
suspended from the ceiling. They know
whose death they grieve, who were themselves

expelled from out of that first small paradise
between their mothers' ovaries. And so
they weep open-mouthed or into their hands,

forgetting shame. John the Younger
can barely hold up his head. The body
in death, so difficult to behold—

the seamed bodice (also red) drawn tight
over the liver's cloudy ampules and perforated
kidneys. Her peasant's feet, unshod and

bloated with edema. Here is the brown and careworn face,
the tangle of hair and its brittle halo, the thickened arms
outstretched along the plank, exhausted fingers—

Fingers still shapely like my mother's, many years ago
when she held me before a camera after Sunday mass,
smoothed her skirt of cotton voile and tossed

her veil and rope of hair behind one shoulder
— so young, so unafraid of what it meant
to have conceived her child out of wedlock.

— for Cresencia Rillera Buccat

Your Hand in My Side

There are things that could make
a believer out of even you: apparitions,
the sun dancing in the trees, a hail of rose
petals, each bearing the pointillist impression
of a bleeding heart like a message written in
invisible ink, held up to the light.
A whole stadium fills with worshippers, armed
with candles thoughtfully stuck in cardboard
discs, to catch droppings of melted wax.
The crowd leans forward as if on one breath
to catch a glimpse of the evangelist's pure white
tuxedo, its sateen panels glinting like carved ice.

Now come forward and witness, booms
the voice on loudspeakers, and you want to fling
yourself on your knees and hobble all the way
to the altar, where an old man is scrambling
upright from his wheelchair, and another
has thrown away his hearing aid. Someone
has fallen prostrate, babbling in tongues—
and you want to be close enough to hear if
what's said is lucid, without need for translation.

But at the communion rail people steer clear of you
because you forget to stick out your tongue
at the right moment; you hesitate to take
the scented hanky for wiping the public spittle
off the statue's base, before bending to reverently kiss
the plaster foot that grinds the serpent's head
to chalky bits. Are you your own worst undoing?

Still, there must be some use for that uncertain figure
in all the books and sacred pictures, the one
we don't see clearly because all our attention, till now,
has focused on the hero who's blessed surely
not just with faith but with nerves of steel to act on it.
Choose, says the voice; unerringly, the hand touches
one of only two doorknobs and *voilá,* it opens
onto the herb garden, not the one that yields
a pit of snakes or den of hungry lions.

Who *is* that figure, hanging back a little and shifting
her weight from foot to foot, the one who asks
too many questions like what was the name of Lot's
wife anyway, and why did she look back?
There must have been a compelling reason,
not the least of them the knowledge that she had
daughters, so how could she just walk on, leave them
behind in that rain of sulfur and fire? But for her
betrayal, she's turned into this handful of crystals
I swirl and swirl in a salt cellar, a rhythmical
music that's fitting accompaniment to my own
examinations of conscience.

And there is Thomas, demanding empirical proof,
wanting to poke and probe the punctured flesh;
to measure the distances traveled by the body
in its fall and resuscitation. What gives me hope
is that he's dealt with more gently, suffering only
a mild public rebuke after satisfying the need to mess
with evidence, like a child who just wants to finger-paint
when all the rest have graduated to the mysteries
of cursive writing. For all we know, he is there still,
among jars of bread-colored Play-Doh, turning
the cleverly modeled limbs, now clean and without
blemish, over and over in wonderment.

I feel him here, too, as your hand in my side, traveling
the length and breadth of me in the night like a compass
verifying latitudes and the presence of land, an anchor
for the otherwise errant heart. I dream of Thomas
and his mission, Thomas the not completely faithless.
True to the habits of this world, he fiddles
with pendulums, spectroscopes, and light meters,
muttering without guile under his breath about ways
to capture the movement of alpha particles on film.

Sometimes I worry about him. Spying a field
of mushrooms, perhaps the prized *Royal Agaric*
which occurs in a genus containing some of the most
poisonous gill fungi known, he'll probably want to test
each one himself. He'll sprint ahead of the joggers
and nannies pushing strollers, gather the slender
yellow stalks and their smooth, beautiful cups in one hand,
even as he nibbles chunks of the *Destroying Angel*
in the other— stumbling up the walk, gasping
warnings that passersby will fail to read as ungainly testament
of love, that struggle with the unruly chaos of matter and belief.

IV /

POSTCARDS FROM THE WHITE CITY

BLUR

To cherish the photograph, to bathe it in fluids, engrave
    it with light. The soul wavers in the interstices,

forever undeveloped. *Dear ___, I send you this picture*
    as a remembrance. As you can see the costume cannot disguise

I am a woman from the mountains. A woman in a skirt
    of paneled silk, dark hair down to the backs of her knees,

points of her triangular shawl gathered in one hand and the other
    posed against a pedestal's base,

supporting a rain of flowers.
    Nothing in the photographer's studio suggests

the ruins outside: loosened gates of the city, stone
    bridges and low-rise buildings crumbled into gravel.

Bodies floating downriver; pale, glistening
    and wreathed among the fish and rushes. One face

shy of the ethereal, the faces of purchased idols— *Tricycle driver*
    in faded pantaloons. Woman vendor in native

dress. Grandmother and spittoon. Child and mother
    with distended breasts. Three women on the steps

picking hair-lice. Seven earthenware pots balanced on the head. The cheirization,
    the coolness of the caption— *Antes y despues los terremotos,* late 1880s—

surprising and electric, the obliterated tremor. The face
    that swims to the surface, still mouthing its desires.

ALBOROTOS

Early autumn, Virginia. Cello
of insects at the windowpane. The last
magnolias drop their clutch of matches,
their spent perfume sticks. Their skirts
loosen and turn caramel, color of *café
con leche* into which my grandmother also
dropped the breakfast eggs to boil. *Thrift,*
she said, sucking in her cheeks as she lit
her *cigarillo* in the stove's gas flame.
Sometimes, on cold mornings, it was
the glowing end she clamped in her mouth.

*

For sale in a shop one day: mint tins and old Alhambra cigar boxes—
hinged, shellacked, beaded and strung on leather cords. The past as chic
scriptorium, a small valise into which now only a few items will fit:
lipstick, compact, lighter, a box of *kreteks* or *gauloises.*
The old-time smell of calamity erased.

*

Disembarking at Pulkovo airport, a hallucinatory
moment— *What is that,* I asked, sniffing the air.
The woman who had come to meet me said *Chto
ty imeesh' vvidu?* Later that week, in my room at the inn,
the toilet handle broke. A plumber in blue coveralls
came to fix it. He smoked and sang, clattered tools
and smoked. The housekeepers came to change
linens and vacuum the carpet. The light at night
remained the same as day. Trying to write at my desk,
I wondered if I was the distortion. I imagined myself
crossing a damp courtyard, sitting under a tree,
raising two fingers and a cupped hand to my mouth.

*

My neighbors are laying out adobe
on their walk, raking leaves in their back
lot, burning them in the shadow of the elm.
Wood smoke and leaf-mold smudge
the air. I ask if they know about tobacco
plantations, how Virginia Tobacco
wound up in the islands— The company
taught women and girls to plant in rows,
to gather and dry the broad leaves and grade
them for rolling. Picture them in clean
cotton skirts and white blouses, kerchiefs
tied around their heads: sorting, rolling, packing.
The smell would not rinse from their skins.

*

When the women led a strike, at first
the company scoffed and called it a dismissive word
that meant something like a tantrum, instead of
the beginning of a revolution.

Postcards from the White City

Meet me in St. Louis, Louis
Meet me at the fair,
Don't tell me the lights are shining
Any place but there;
We will dance the Hoochee-Koochee
I will be your tootsie-wootsie
If you will meet me in St. Louis, Louis
Meet me at the Fair.
          — "Meet Me in St. Louis"

World's Fair, St. Louis, Missouri; 1904

Here, where we were almost nothing,
on the banks of the Arrowhead River
they mapped the unruly forest, laid down
promenades and columns. Lights flickered
from dusk to dawn, their arctic glow eating
at the cone of darkness. The darkness was to become
extinct. Was to perish. The previous year, the first
flight in Kitty Hawk, North Carolina.
The first time a girl tiptoed round-mouthed
and pulled the cord that tripped
a light switch on— In Lancaster, Kentucky
she watched as her hands washed themselves
in light, blue like gentian violet, their shadows
swimming like a pair of fish.

World's Fair, St. Louis, Missouri; 1904

In Paris, Vienna, New York, street lamps
dispute nocturnal authority. Along
avenues and bridges, since the late 1800s,
orange flares crown the ends of coiled filaments—
tiny as cloves, riven into the base of a socket.
We learn by degrees about this light. The eye
understands how butter limns the edge of a knife
to make it seem less dangerous. Blinking, I stepped
out of train doors. Across the platform a boy
tended a kettle; the wind smelled of damp wood, hot
chestnuts. It is told that two of our number lay down
in a boxcar and died as simply as two pears might
tip over in their tissue-lined carton. *Inevitable,* they said.
Frost in April, the ground still salted over with snow.

World's Fair, St. Louis, Missouri; 1904

Bridge of Spain, moss-spackled corridor
of war; decayed wisteria. Among divided
flowers, a riot of bees. Axis of invisible
lines. In some museums your lover can stand
beneath a cupola— whispers unnerve,
lick at the ear like a mouth, meaning
to arouse capitulation. Wings
disappear behind the walled city, tearing
the luminous air. Who remembers forty-seven
acres, villages radiating from a central plaza?
I am drawn to the edges, to undisciplined
life in swamps, in markets not yet fallen
to the catalogue— Where might I find such
fruit as that passing tourist savors with her lips?

Smithsonian Institution; Summer 2002

What are the soft parts of the body? Everything
to be foraged. Deed of sale, threshing floor.
The nails might be gathered from their beds, a hair-
plait carefully snipped and laid in a hinged box.
What of fingers and breasts, distended with weight?
The heart and spleen, amphora of bile. Tongue
and tonsil, the lip's garnet-colored cleft
to study just like tagged and numbered fish.
Chaff from grain, repeated motion of the hand,
winnowing. This one knew how the fermented
gleanings were sweet to the gods, droplets shaken
on the ground among itinerant chickens.
Such patient scratching in the stones. Who'll find
the white medallions of the dissected body?

Musuem of Science and Industry; Spring 2003

Underneath plaster moldings, old barns,
stables; plain masonry, blocks of factory space.
Rafters where finches once scattered in a panic
of light. Marvelous façades applied in layers—
so the white glare of buildings rendered smoke
glasses an absolute necessity.
The muses of science and industry
press marbled foreheads against the pitched
roof. Scrolls flutter down the length of pillars
by the entryway; crowds thicken
on the esplanades, lining up for tickets.
In the galleries, a low monsoon hum—
camera shutters whirring open and close.
In rooms where lamps are shaded with mica
bodies hang from walls, robed in dusky brown.

St. Louis, Missouri; 1904

> *. . . the imprint of an oar upon the water.*
> — Kate Chopin (1850–1904)

Muted vibrato of insects at night.
Sometimes we worked by moonlight, lashing reeds
and fronds for walls and roofs. By day the men
cleared campground, searched under guard for river
stones. How to explain the need for sacrifice—
a hog's singed hide, white beneath rendered fat?
When it rains our lean-tos rustle. From riverbanks,
the gurgled descant of frogs and geckos.
It's almost familiar, until we turn—
banded lights in the distance, the visible
edge of the great wheel and its rocking gondolas.
I think I hear its joints creak in the wind—
cables looped in midair, describing
our brittle revolutions in place.

World's Fair, St. Louis, Missouri; 1904

The girl at the end of our table tossed stray
curls over one shoulder. "In all of this,
what is at stake?" she asked with petulance.
I suspect already she'd taken pleasure
at the sideshows where dogs devoured white
mice, and a woman in a Victorian pompadour
spun onstage with a chair clenched in her teeth.
I'd like to have drawn her deeper in, drop
her on a buckskin hide with instructions:
Instead of Geronimo, how about you
fill this exhibit hall with miniature bows
and blunted arrows? They'll sell for copper
coins before sundown. In darkness you'll covet
each firstborn never seen, signed away in contract.

St. Petersburg; Summer 2003

Here in another city washed by white
nights that will not set, I sit in a window's bay
framed by copper curtains, a veil of doubled
glass from which to look upon the mustard
yellow buildings. Across the street, a gallery
of artifacts and disjointed gestures.
Child's chair balanced on a wide sill. One floor
above, a woman intimate at her toilette,
the tips of her nipples swabbed with a patina
of lamplight. A shoulder brushed and highlighted,
returned to the shadows. In the next room,
someone hangs a string bag by the window.
Red shaft of an anthurium peeled away
from its green plate. How swiftly things corrode.

St. Petersburg; Summer 2003

". . . city of spectral light"

Nearly a hundred years from the ethnography
exhibit, I walk in Dostoyevsky's old neighborhood.
Oblivious to passing traffic, faded
Ladas and tourist buses, two teenage girls
scrape the corner with skates and then are gone.
Stayed executions, forced labor, this city's
pastel stones raised by the dying with bare
hands. A marble plaque beneath a window marks
how high the waterline in the great flood of
1824. Windows anchored by persistent scrolls
so histories meet in the audible moment.
In the Haymarket, in the air above the Neva,
pukh loosened from poplar trees like snow
in summer, white drifts converging overhead.

Yekaterinsky dvorets, Tsarkovoe Selo; Summer 2003

All morning we waited, spoke in the rain
under steaming umbrellas, of monuments
and shrines along the road. We lent our coats
to others. Wind stroked the curved courtyard pink
with gravel. Later, behind massive doors,
our feet in soot-colored slippers, wheels
clicked and turned. We blinked at outlines, at shadows
and illuminations. One face refracted
in mirrors and gilded panels, one knocked
its bones on cabinets with inlaid roses.
Parlors gashed with crimson, crumpled green foil;
and then one room where the white ruched curtains
became mottled skin, became ferrous oxide,
resin. I paused on the threshold, the broken carapace.

Flower seller, Haymarket; Summer 2003

Dear ___, we walked today, a group of ten,
to the Haymarket, careful to avoid
potholes filled with last night's rain. A flower
seller stood beneath an awning faded pink.
She hardly blinked in her apron striped coral
and yellow against a field of severe black,
when cameras aimed and shot. We waited
our turn to duck under the archway and cross
the courtyard hung with laundry, then climb four
flights of stairs. The past is intimate here
as an ex-lover sighted in an airport lounge,
a cat that darts from out of nowhere and rubs
against your calf just as you're fingering graffiti
carved on the wall: *Rodya, no, please don't do it.*

MRS. WILKIN TEACHES AN IGOROT THE CAKEWALK

Missouri Historical Society, Photographer unknown; 1904

> *. . . new-caught sullen peoples,*
> *Half devil and half child.*
> — Rudyard Kipling

The path was raked dust, brittle pods, thistle burr,
gravel pushed to the edges to clear a surface

level as frosting. One-two, she led with a foot
and one extended arm to harness

the metronome at my wrist. Oh I could smell
fear and loneliness on the margins of the constructed

gardens. Under the trellis, the shadow of my dying
took up a gong and danced. I was a mystery, applauded

as charming. *God's children, God's own little children,* she cried.
I heard the sound of river water gather in the mouth of

a gramophone. What does it matter, now that I am in this world?
She led me by the hand. We were

the animal brought to prance before the gods.
In this diorama, I longed for the sight of one rice bird,

one crooked terrace stone. The cameo around her neck
glowed, dark moon over apron fields and asphalt.

HILL STATION

Baguio City, Philippines

> *We found conditions exactly as described in the Spanish report. . . .*
> *It took us but a short time to decide that here was an ideal site for a future city. . . .*
> *[T]here were scores of places where, in order to have a beautiful house lot, one*
> *needed only to construct driveways and go to work with a lawnmower.*
> — Dean C. Worcester, Secretary of the Interior, 1898,
> *The Philippine Islands and their people: a record of personal*
> *observation and experience with a short summary of the*
> *more important facts in the history of the archipelago*

These are the woods through which they came— at the turn
of the last century, riding ponies from base camp, where the rail-
road could not climb further. Cutting through virgin

brush and green pine so thick the fragrance
reminded them of New England, thousands of miles
away. *All one needs is a map and a lawnmower,* exulted Dean

Worcester in his journals, between ornithology
notes. Migrant birds arrive from sojourning in far-off
islands, punctual as November and its haul of sun-

flowers. But the pine is thinner today, above Burnham Park
where a bust of the Chicago architect stands, its bronze
nose shiny as a beacon-flare pinning this city down

in hollow rock and limestone. I can walk
from the City Hall and pathways around the man-
made lake the size of a large duck-pond,

past the soccer field and grandstand, up
Session Road, named by American officials who sat
in session every summer, fleeing the choking heat,

mosquitoes and malaria of the provinces.
They would not give up their top hats,
their cravats; their coat-tails, waistcoats

and wool trousers; their wives, those yards of skirts
and heavy petticoats. They gave the native
girls their first white blouses; a Christian gesture,

they stressed— embarrassed by the abundance of brown
breasts, bosoms paganly adorned with layers of onyx
and carnelian, smoky agate, gold leaf and traded shells,

polished to brittleness. You see such heirlooms now
only in antique shops, wrapped in oilcloth or resting
in the shallow lips of food baskets. Mothers bring them

to exchange for cash, thinking of daughters and sons
anxious to leave the mountains, thinking of new
things they might become: teachers, lawyers, even doctors

or nurses in that other land, America. And I can walk
further east, toward rows of wooden cottages with stone
chimneys on Cabinet Hill, arranged on a rise— reminder

of the summer we took a trolley tour of Washington:
the guide drove us downhill through Embassy Row,
our heads spinning like tennis balls as she volleyed

and served from left to right and back, naming
the flags of countries that fluttered on each side of
the street. The neatly painted houses with their trim

gardens and hedges, this country of precisely
numbered doors, the solid names of streets— Jackson,
Monroe, Jefferson, Adams— the same I saw

repeated reassuringly in every city: New York,
Chicago, San Francisco, and all the small
midwestern towns I visited between. Boys

in my fourth grade class had names like Monroe Gawigawen
and Jefferson Palpallatoc. They were of Igorot stock, again
what you might call *native*. Other children taunted them,

those who thought themselves more citified, more cleansed of
savage origins. Monroe had a limp. I hear he sports long hair and has
become a human rights lawyer. I do not know what happened to Jefferson.

DESCENT

In 1904 more than eleven hundred indigenous Filipinos were transported to
St. Louis, Missouri, to serve as live exhibits at the World's Fair and Exposition.

Far from the province of
    beginnings, I can acknowledge my face

has finally begun to resemble the canvas it feared
    most. But I remember how it was to feel my way

down mountain trails, drink from hair-lined throats of plants, sleep
    crouched among the fiddlehead fern. Three days, five,

then the canopy lightened. I walked past clearings where crops
    had taken hold: sweet potato and beans trained to the stake,

runners and tendrils curling toward commerce in the markets. Even before
    I saw the first few shingled houses, unhappy dogs

tethered to their posts smelled my approach. Faces gawked
    as I walked past. To them I was a stranger,

dark and not to be trusted; my woven skirt a red-striped
    carnival tent that might open to what they

could not imagine— though I'd spent my whole life until then,
    no farther away than where they might glance

at the sun lowering itself at the horizon, between notched
    limestones; a few moments of convulsive light, mother-

of-pearl sheen, ripple of cream, stroke that primes the canvas
    before darkness closes around the world like a bead.

*

Detached figure, I walked to the bay where crowds gathered around fishing
    nets. Flies hovered above their heads, dark wings gold-tipped

like doors of miniature tabernacles, though this was before the *time of my saving*
    and instruction. The heat, threaded with salt and moist as a mouth,

made me swoon. What I desired: to hoist myself over the side
    of the first vessel I saw, lie down in its shadowed hold, as if

the lap-lap, lap-lap of water would take me to you. But my purpose
    was intercepted. Someone came forward, guided me across a road,

into the town. *Whereto?* I did not know, but at that time I believed
    all paths would make themselves plain again so I could find my way.

I slept and woke. In a glass, a woman brought me the milk of an animal
    and made me drink. I rose from my pallet in the night and shat in the garden

under a *manzanilla* tree until my sweat was warm again, unclammy.

*

A season passed. We stayed a few months in that town, and then another
    just like the one to which I made my way when first I left our village.

The man I worked for took pictures— some landscapes, farm houses
    and crosshatched dwellings; they sighed a little

as ethers in the tray affixed their souls to paper. A few of wildlife:
    a bird with its breast rouged as though from harm, one lost

cloud-rat before it skittered away toward the forest.
    It came to me his interest was people that in some way resembled me

as I resembled them. He loved our habit: the tiny bells that women dangled
    from belts of plaited horsehair, their combs of polished wood,

boxes where areca nut and leaves are stored for chew, their insides stained
    the same wild red as spit. He loved their deformities and rituals:

he catalogued the splayed toes and claw-feet of grandfathers, earlobes distended
    by pipes and padlocks; folds of skin, fingers troubling a pig's spleen

for omens, horoscopes. His wife had me help in the maintenance
    of their world: buying food from white or lowland traders, boiling

to render safe for consumption; mending the *worn but goodly*
    linens. It was she instructed me and sought to baptize me, secretly

afraid of words I mumbled in dreams, in my own
    language. Husband, even then I dogged your shadow in my sleep.

I learned to wear shoes on my feet. Garments covered my breasts and arms,
    and these I took off only when, eventually, I posed for him—

my dark breasts artfully concealed under an arrangement of necklaces,
      agate and carnelian. I came to understand their talk, their gestures

and nuances. I was cook and laundress, subject, apprentice, their
      surrogate. They praised me *like a daughter.*

In the sun, I whitened clothes. I ripened
      beside the honeysuckle, tending my time.

The Philippine Reservation at the 1904 World's Fair and Exposition in St. Louis, Missouri, was laid out across forty-seven acres near the Arrowhead River. The cost for building it, as well as for transporting over eleven hundred indigenous Filipinos from the islands, amounted to more than a million dollars and was financed by the American Government and its colonial branch in the Philippines. The Filipino bodies at the fair made up half—and the largest—contingent of native bodies. Live exhibits of Filipinos, Ainu, Native American Indians, and pygmies, were meant to illustrate the development of nations from savagery to civilization, and America's role as a new imperial power.

WHITE NIGHTS

St. Petersburg, Russia

— *after Akhmatova*

Between the paired gryphons with golden wings
    and the people on the bridge
Between the tenderness of cables that slice their mouths of stone
Between the silence under peeling wallpaper and the sounds
        of several commodes flushing in the night—

Between the river water and reflected light below
Between the river and the swell of foreign consonants
Between the box of burlap stage slippers and the ancient doors
        of the Theatrical Museum—

At last I dream of your face without remorse.

WHEN I THINK OF THE TIME I THINK OF NARRATIVE,

condensation that forms a line of drops
across windows so a finger could draw connections—

A face leaning close, as close as one
could hover next to another to propose
a point from which to begin—

            And so it begins,
the traveling line that can only carry so much
in terms of revelation. A movement or suggestion,
which the hand follows then augments
in part from force of habit, because it wants to see
what gathers, what form of completion.

The water resists this type of writing,
insists on the story it wants to tell.

Or is this its lesson,
what's fallen these many days from the sky
without remorse or apology, not even a covenant;
what washes roofs and pavements with equal regard?

O rain,
whose only real gesture is liquid and falling,
which sends people home through the swell of evening
traffic and on to the comfort of dinners and beds.

A man crosses from one end of the city to another,
carrying a book or a letter.

A hand dips a metal plate into a bath of salts and acids.
The images focus and come into view.

LUISA A. IGLORIA

is an associate professor in the MFA creative writing program at Old Dominion University. The winner of numerous national and international creative writing awards, she is the author of nine books.

Lightning Source UK Ltd.
Milton Keynes UK
UKHW012259010821
388087UK00001B/20

9 780268 031787